T5-BSG-354

CHRISTMAS SOLOS

B♭ TRUMPET

How to use the CD Accompaniment:
A melody cue appears on the right channel only. If your CD player has a balance adjustment,
you can adjust the volume of the melody by turning down the right channel.

ISBN 0-634-03851-6

HAL•LEONARD®
CORPORATION
7777 W. BLUEMOUND RD. P.O. BOX 13819 MILWAUKEE, WI 53213

Visit Hal Leonard Online at
www.halleonard.com

ANGELS WE HAVE HEARD ON HIGH

Trumpet

BRING A TORCH, JEANNETTE, ISABELLA

Trumpet

THE COVENTRY CAROL

Trumpet

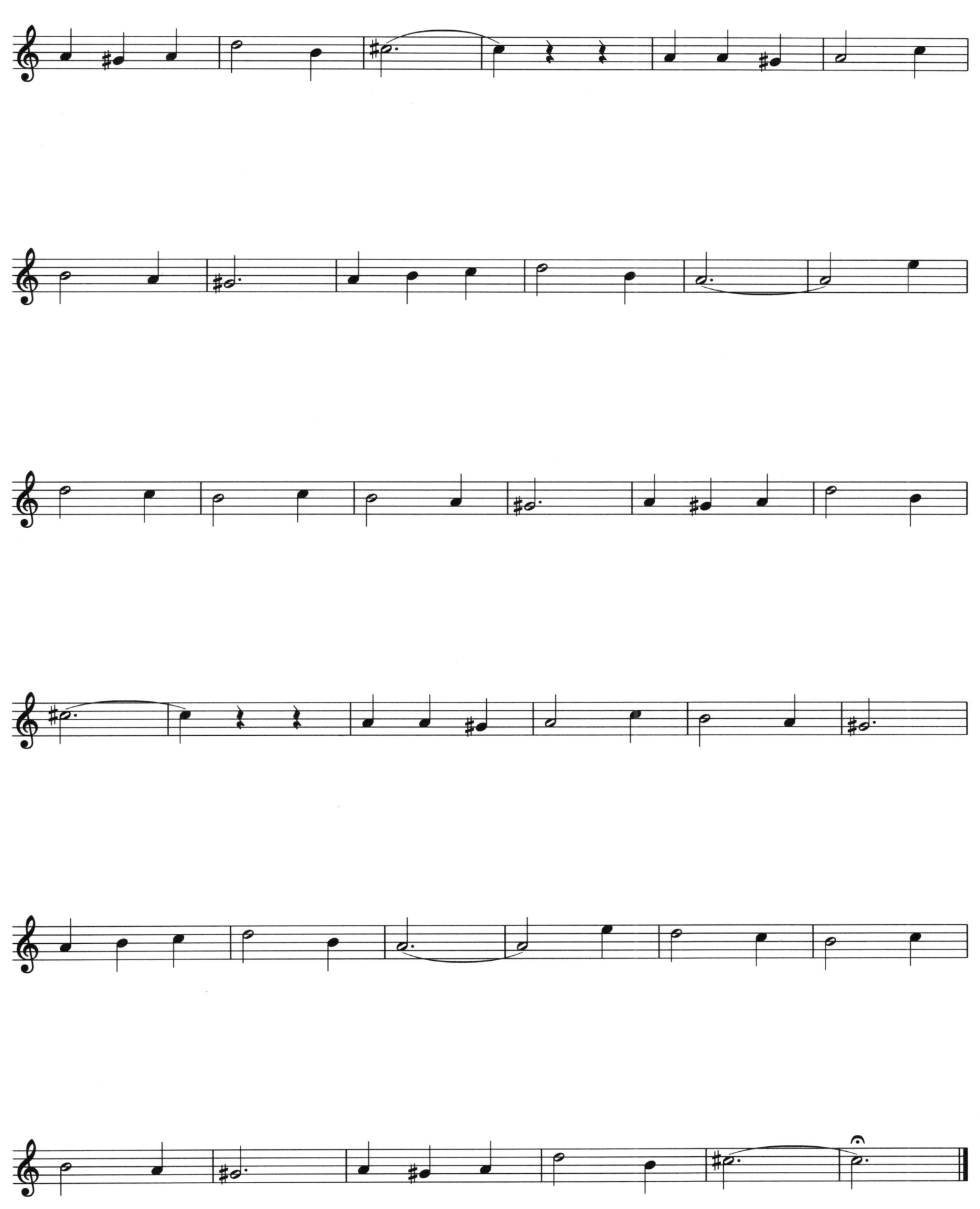

GOD REST YE MERRY, GENTLEMEN

Trumpet

THE HOLLY AND THE IVY

Trumpet

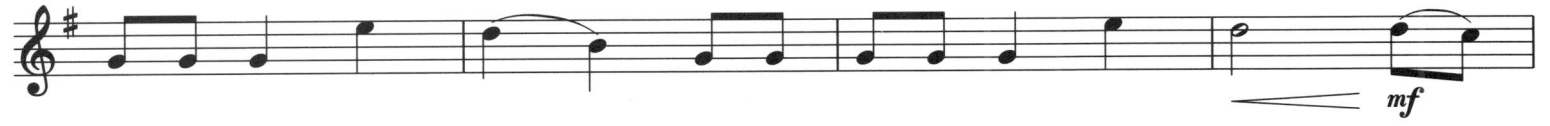

O HOLY NIGHT

Trumpet

SILENT NIGHT

Trumpet

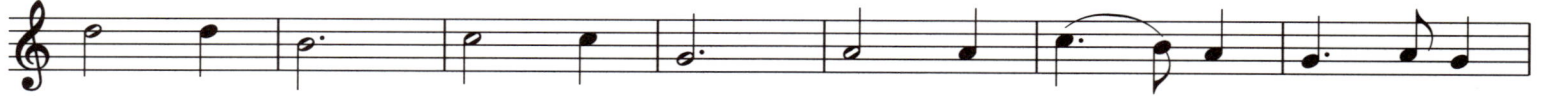

WHAT CHILD IS THIS?

Trumpet

mf

rit.

O COME, O COME, EMMANUEL

Trumpet